GEOFF BOYCOTT'S BOOK FOR YOUNG CRICKETERS

Stanley Paul
London Melbourne Sydney Auckland Johannesburg

Acknowledgments

The author acknowledges with thanks the help he has received from Terry Brindle, Sports Media Ltd, Art and Design Limited, Bill Ireland, Andrew Whittuck and Patrick Eagar in the preparation of this book.

Stanley Paul & Co. Ltd

An imprint of the Hutchinson Publishing Group

3 Fitzroy Square, London WIP 6JD

Hutchinson Group (Australia) Pty Ltd
30–32 Cremorne Street, Richmond South, Victoria 3121
PO Box 151, Broadway, New South Wales 2007

Hutchinson Group (NZ) Ltd
32–34 View Road, PO Box 40–086, Glenfield, Auckland 10

Hutchinson Group (SA) (Pty) Ltd
PO Box 337, Bergvlei 2012, South Africa

First published 1976
Reprinted 1977, 1978, 1979, 1980

© Geoff Boycott 1976

Photographs © Patrick Eagar, Press Association,
Syndication International, Central Press,
Ken Kelly, Sport & General

Printed in Great Britain by The Anchor
Press Ltd and bound by Wm Brendon & Son Ltd
both of Tiptree, Essex

ISBN (P) 0 09 126931 8

Contents

Preface

Geoff Boycott in his great period was the finest batsman in the world; certainly the most dedicated. His batting bears the stamp of careful analysis and construction of method. His right hand is low on the bat, the left effectively high; the left does, positively, lead while the right provides the main propulsive force; and it is all done with quite unusually complete balance of power. His first movement is back and across. He is a careful assessor of the ball, with the great batsman's gift of rarely being in error as to whether to go forward or back. If his batting has one outstanding quality it must be that of quite meticulous placing; he plays through the gaps in a field with greater precision than any other contemporary batsman. The figures of Boycott's batting are convincing enough in themselves; they are even more impressive seen – as in fairness they should be – against the background of his isolation, of the stress and physical battery to which the target batsman is nowadays subjected.

At five feet ten inches, Boycott is of ideal height for a well-balanced batsman: he is firmly but not heavily built, a coherent mover, strong enough for his purpose and conscientiously fit. His batting is thought out, planned to make the most of his abilities while securing him as completely as possible against the perils to which all batsmen are heirs. He bases his technique on a defence organized as near to flawlessness as can be. Indeed, when he is in form he comes so close to ruling out error that it often seems as if he need never be out. He judges swing well, plays spin with genuine understanding and, despite the battering he has had, scores steadily against pace. At the start of an innings he plays himself in without anxiety, not the least worried if he does not score for half an hour while he takes the pace of the pitch and his measure of the bowling. Despite his quick assessment of the bowled ball, he often leaves his stroke quite late, yet without having to hurry it. Then he gradually exerts his range of strokes like a racing motorist opening the throttle and on his great days his batting has an air of inevitability. Geoff Boycott, a superb technician, has – as is well for the team he plays for – an unfailing hunger for batting, runs and success; and his successor is not in sight.

John Arlott

Introduction

Cricket is not an easy game. There are a few fortunate people who seem to take to it and do well without apparent effort but for most of us cricket demands a lot of practice and a willingness to work hard to maintain high standards.

If you want to get to the top or simply play to the best of your ability there is no substitute for practice. Not everyone is cut out to be a county player or reach Test standards but practically everyone who takes up the game can improve his performances by perfecting the basic techniques.

It's never too early to start. I went to a coaching school when I was nine and there have been many good players who started before that. If you can get professional coaching, that's the best way; if you can't there is a lot to be learned from watching good players.

Let me emphasize that I advise anyone to play sport rather than watch. It's nice to see youngsters at cricket matches and I think they should be made welcome, perhaps more welcome than they are at some places. But if you have a choice, be a player rather than a spectator.

When you do watch cricket watch the best players – and with your head as well as your eyes.

You will see they all have differences in style and approach but you may also be surprised how many similarities there are, how many basic rules apply to them all. Ask yourself what a player does and why, see if you can spot the difference between one delivery and the next. If the captain makes a fielding change, see if you can spot the reason. In this way you will learn a great deal and enjoy the match all the more.

After all, enjoyment is what the game is all about. Because a professional cricketer earns his living from the game and has an additional responsibility to provide entertainment, he probably takes his pleasures more seriously than the man who plays purely for relaxation. So it should be.

But Sir Donald Bradman once said: 'If the game is not enjoyed, why bother to play it at all?' It took me a while to appreciate the value of that philosophy, but I recommend it to anyone.

Cricket can be something of an inconvenient game because it is time-consuming. Even cricket on the village green usually demands a full afternoon – unless, of course, somebody comes up with a demon bowling performance or one of the umpires has to catch an early bus. But the fact that cricketers are brought together for longish periods helps breed a unique sense of friendship and involvement – not just between team-mates but among rival teams.

This is certainly so in county cricket and local cricket has a special social atmosphere unlike any other game. It's a great way to spend your time.

I am often asked which performances have given me most pleasure over the years and it's not an easy question to answer. Batting well on a difficult wicket for a modest-looking score can be as satisfying as hitting hundreds, but some achievements obviously do stick in the mind.

My first century for Yorkshire was especially sweet because it was scored in a Roses match when we were struggling a bit. The 1965 Gillette Cup final when I scored 146 and helped Brian Close put on 192 against Surrey will always rank high in my memory; then there was that wonderful tour of Australia in 1970–1 when we brought back the Ashes. I have mixed memories about that because I was injured, but it was a great tour.

My first match for England, being asked to captain Yorkshire, averaging 100 in a first-class season and scoring centuries against every other county and Test country – those are some of the other achievements which have given me pleasure over the years. I hope there will be a lot more.

One thing is certain – nobody will ever achieve really good, consistent performances unless he masters the basics of the game. And the higher you go up cricket's ladder, the more important that becomes.

When I am struggling to find form – and that happens to everyone at some time or another – I concentrate hard on getting the so-called simple things right. I am never afraid to go back to basics because that is where every good performance begins.

This book sets out to help you master the basic ingredients of cricket. I hope you find it interesting and helpful. Work hard at the game and it will repay you in many hours of enjoyment and a real sense of achievement. Believe me, it really is worth the effort.

Geoff Boycott

Batting

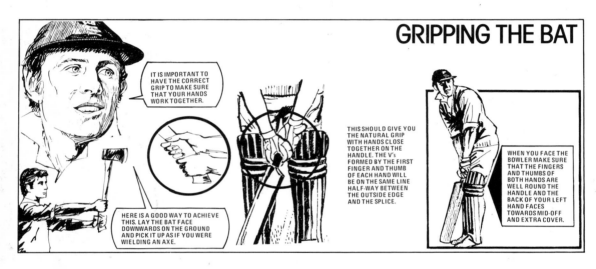

The beginning of every good innings. Comfortable, balanced and alert without being tense – a good stance has an air of permanence about it, as the 1973 New Zealanders discovered at Headingley.

TAKING GUARD

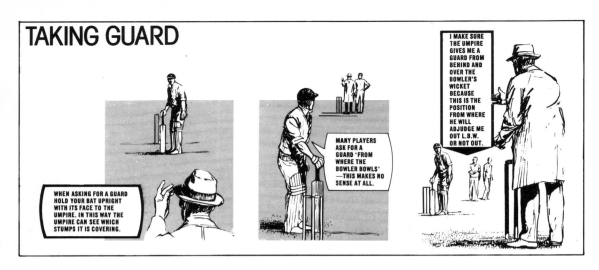

I MAKE SURE THE UMPIRE GIVES ME A GUARD FROM BEHIND AND OVER THE BOWLER'S WICKET BECAUSE THIS IS THE POSITION FROM WHERE HE WILL ADJUDGE ME OUT L.B.W. OR NOT OUT.

MANY PLAYERS ASK FOR A GUARD 'FROM WHERE THE BOWLER BOWLS' —THIS MAKES NO SENSE AT ALL.

WHEN ASKING FOR A GUARD HOLD YOUR BAT UPRIGHT WITH ITS FACE TO THE UMPIRE. IN THIS WAY THE UMPIRE CAN SEE WHICH STUMPS IT IS COVERING.

THE BACK LIFT

A VITAL PART OF ALL BATTING STROKES IS THE BACKLIFT. REMEMBER THE STRAIGHTER YOUR BACKLIFT THE BETTER CHANCE YOU HAVE OF PLAYING THE BALL WITH A STRAIGHT BAT. HERE I HAVE PICKED UP MY BAT OVER THE TOP OF THE STUMPS.

THE LEFT ARM AND WRIST DO NEARLY ALL THE WORK. NOTICE HOW MY BAT IS TAKEN BACK BY MY LEFT HAND AND THE FACE OF THE BAT OPENS TOWARDS POINT.

LIFTING THE BAT BACK IS NOT NATURAL AND IT REQUIRES HARD WORK TO GET IT RIGHT. I USED TO PRACTICE MY BACK LIFT IN FRONT OF A MIRROR AND IT HAS HELPED ME TO KEEP A STRAIGHT BAT.

KEEP A STRAIGHT BAT

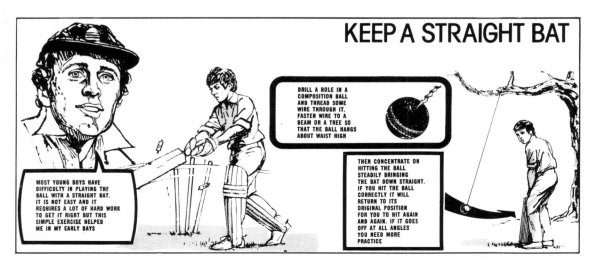

DRILL A HOLE IN A COMPOSITION BALL AND THREAD SOME WIRE THROUGH IT. FASTEN WIRE TO A BEAM OR A TREE SO THAT THE BALL HANGS ABOUT WAIST HIGH

THEN CONCENTRATE ON HITTING THE BALL STEADILY BRINGING THE BAT DOWN STRAIGHT. IF YOU HIT THE BALL CORRECTLY IT WILL RETURN TO ITS ORIGINAL POSITION FOR YOU TO HIT AGAIN AND AGAIN. IF IT GOES OFF AT ALL ANGLES YOU NEED MORE PRACTICE

MOST YOUNG BOYS HAVE DIFFICULTY IN PLAYING THE BALL WITH A STRAIGHT BAT. IT IS NOT EASY AND IT REQUIRES A LOT OF HARD WORK TO GET IT RIGHT BUT THIS SIMPLE EXERCISE HELPED ME IN MY EARLY DAYS

Master stroke – Colin Cowdrey, one of the most stylish players in the game before his retirement last year, plays a beautifully straight bat against the Australians in Sydney.

PLAYING FORWARD DEFENSIVELY

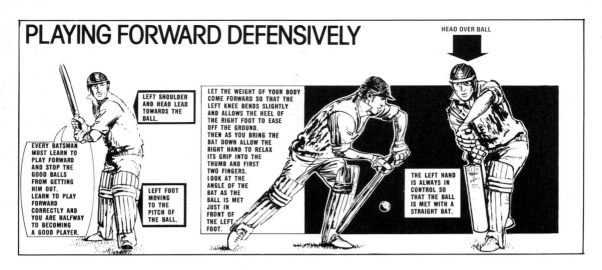

PLAYING BACK DEFENSIVELY

Eyes down, head over ball, weight transferred onto front foot. Play this shot well and you are halfway to becoming a good player.

THE ON DRIVE

THIS IS ONE OF THE MOST DIFFICULT STROKES FOR YOUNG PLAYERS TO MASTER. MAKE SURE THAT YOU TURN AND DIP YOUR LEFT SHOULDER TOWARDS MID-ON. IT WILL NATURALLY FOLLOW THAT YOUR LEFT FOOT WILL OPEN OUT SO THAT THE TOES ARE POINTING DOWN THE PITCH!

NOW WATCH AS MY LEFT KNEE BENDS HOW THE WEIGHT OF MY BODY IS TRANSFERRED ONTO MY LEFT FOOT AND I HIT THE BALL JUST INSIDE MY LEFT TOE.

HERE WITH MY LEFT HAND IN FULL CONTROL I FOLLOW THROUGH WITH A STRAIGHT BAT TOWARDS MID-ON.

THE OFF DRIVE

THE MOST IMPORTANT POINT ABOUT THIS SHOT IS THE MOVEMENT OF THE LEFT SHOULDER WHICH SHOULD TURN AND POINT TOWARDS EXTRA COVER. BY KEEPING YOUR HEAD CLOSE TO THE LEFT SHOULDER YOUR EYES LOOK DOWN ON THE LINE OF THE BALL.

REMEMBER THE WIDER THE BALL THE MORE YOU TURN YOUR BACK ON THE BOWLER. IN THIS WAY YOU MAKE SURE YOU STAY SIDEWAYS ON AND GET YOUR LEFT FOOT TO THE PITCH OF THE BALL.

NOW WITH THE WEIGHT FIRMLY ON THE LEFT FOOT BOTH ARMS FOLLOW THROUGH THE LINE OF THE STROKE.

ATTACKING OFF THE BACK FOOT

WRONG

IT SHOULD BE EASY TO HIT AN ATTACKING BACK FOOT SHOT AFTER LEARNING TO PLAY BACK DEFENSIVELY. BUT YOUNG PLAYERS FIND THIS THE MOST DIFFICULT SHOT TO PLAY BECAUSE THEY WILL TRY TO HIT THE BALL TOO HARD. THIS MEANS THEY THROW THE HEAD BACK AND SCOOP THE BALL UP IN THE AIR.

BE SURE TO MAKE THE MOST OF YOUR HEIGHT BY RISING ON THE TOES OF YOUR RIGHT FOOT AS I DO. THEN WITH THE LEFT HAND CONTROLLING THE SHOT, PUNCH AT THE BALL WITH THE RIGHT HAND JUST BEFORE IMPACT. FORCE IS NOT REQUIRED—THE POWER COMES FROM TIMING.

STILL KEEPING THE HEAD DOWN LET THE BAT FOLLOW THROUGH IN THE DIRECTION OF THE BALL.

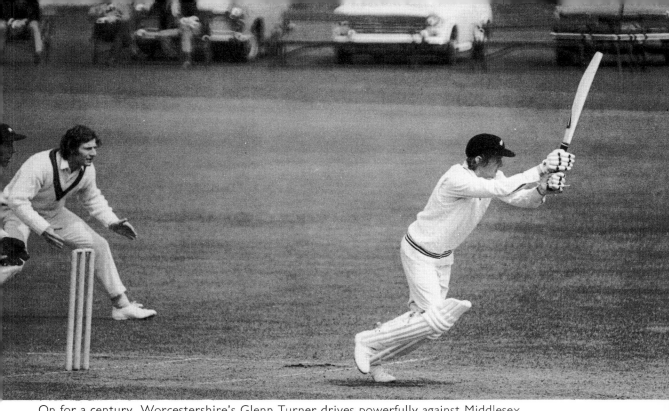

On for a century, Worcestershire's Glenn Turner drives powerfully against Middlesex.

And off the back foot, an attractive stroke in which control and timing are more important than force.

THE SQUARE CUT

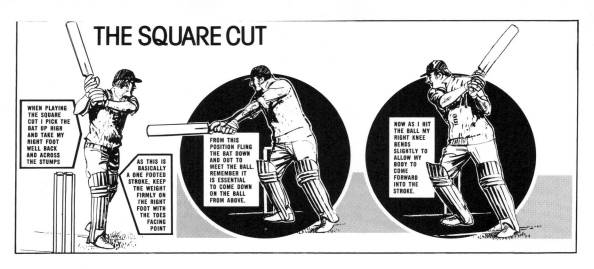

WHEN PLAYING THE SQUARE CUT I PICK THE BAT UP HIGH AND TAKE MY RIGHT FOOT WELL BACK AND ACROSS THE STUMPS

AS THIS IS BASICALLY A ONE FOOTED STROKE, KEEP THE WEIGHT FIRMLY ON THE RIGHT FOOT WITH THE TOES FACING POINT

FROM THIS POSITION FLING THE BAT DOWN AND OUT TO MEET THE BALL. REMEMBER IT IS ESSENTIAL TO COME DOWN ON THE BALL FROM ABOVE.

NOW AS I HIT THE BALL MY RIGHT KNEE BENDS SLIGHTLY TO ALLOW MY BODY TO COME FORWARD INTO THE STROKE.

THE LATE CUT

THE LATE CUT IS A REFINEMENT OF THE SQUARE CUT AND IS USED TO PLACE THE BALL BEHIND THE STUMPS. THERE IS A PRONOUNCED TURN OF THE LEFT SHOULDER AND THE RIGHT FOOT LANDS WELL BACK AND ACROSS THE STUMPS BUT POINTING TO THIRD MAN.

POINTING TO 3rd MAN

I LET THE BALL PASS MY BODY SO THAT IT IS NEARLY LEVEL WITH THE STUMPS BEFORE I MEET IT.

THEN WITH A DOWNWARD MOVEMENT OF THE BAT I DELICATELY STROKE THE BALL. REMEMBER YOU ARE STEERING THE BALL—NOT HITTING IT. THE PACE OF THE BALL WILL HELP IT ON ITS WAY.

CUTTING OFF THE FRONT FOOT

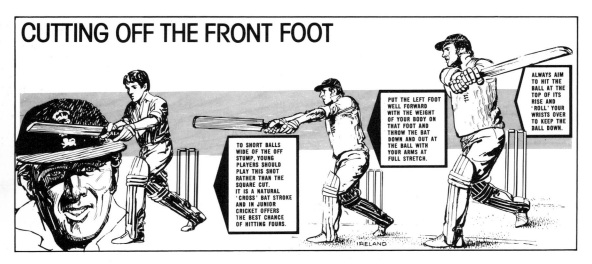

TO SHORT BALLS WIDE OF THE OFF STUMP, YOUNG PLAYERS SHOULD PLAY THIS SHOT RATHER THAN THE SQUARE CUT. IT IS A NATURAL 'CROSS' BAT STROKE AND IN JUNIOR CRICKET OFFERS THE BEST CHANCE OF HITTING FOURS.

PUT THE LEFT FOOT WELL FORWARD WITH THE WEIGHT OF YOUR BODY ON THAT FOOT AND THROW THE BAT DOWN AND OUT AT THE BALL WITH YOUR ARMS AT FULL STRETCH.

ALWAYS AIM TO HIT THE BALL AT THE TOP OF ITS RISE AND 'ROLL' YOUR WRISTS OVER TO KEEP THE BALL DOWN.

Above left Barry Richards, one of the world's most exciting attacking players, puts the force of his body into a fierce square cut – and the smile suggests it beat the field for four.
Above right Left-hander Clive Lloyd cuts fiercely off the front foot on his way to a century in the World Cup final at Lord's.
Below The unkindest and most difficult cut of all as Australia's Greg Chappell steers the ball deftly wide of slip in the second Test in Barbados.

THE SWEEP SHOT

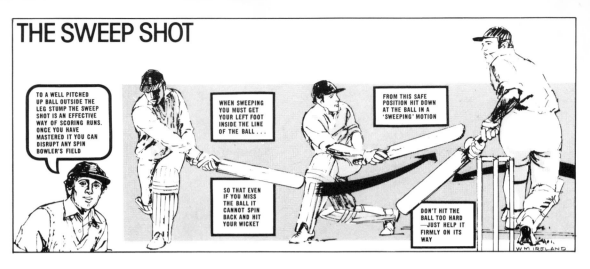

THE PULL SHOT

THE HOOK

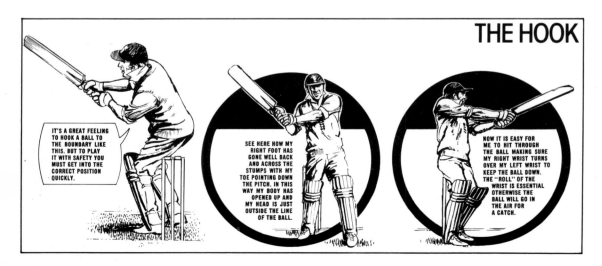

18

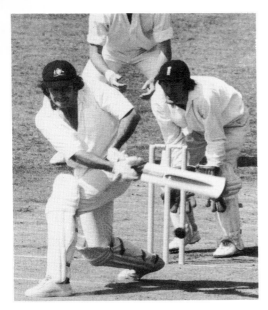

Left Left foot inside the line of the ball, bat sweeping through and down – Ian Chappell's way of dealing with Derek Underwood in the Oval Test against the Australians, 1975.

Middle Pulling out the stops at the Oval.

Bottom I enjoyed that . . . hooking for four is always a great feeling. When the bowler is Dennis Lillee it is extra special.

THE LOFTED STRAIGHT DRIVE

MOVING OUT TO DRIVE

THE STRAIGHT DRIVE

Above left A shot we do not see often enough – South Africa's magnificent Eddie Barlow moving out to drive with perfect balance and co-ordination.

Above right Greg Chappell illustrates perfectly how the arms are used to loft a straight drive.

LEG GLANCE OFF THE FRONT FOOT

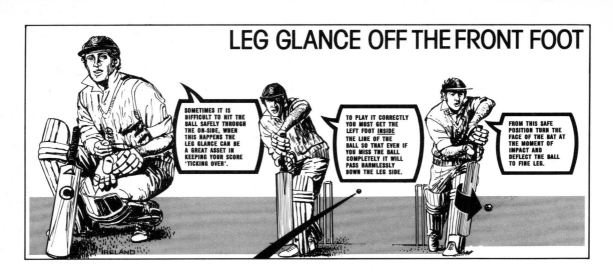

LEG GLANCE OFF THE BACK FOOT

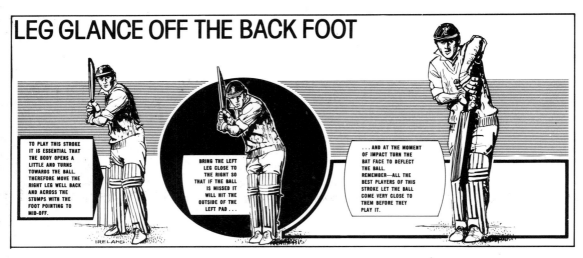

A turn of the wrists at the right moment produces this most delicate shot.

THE FULL TOSS

HITTING A FULL TOSS

YORKERS

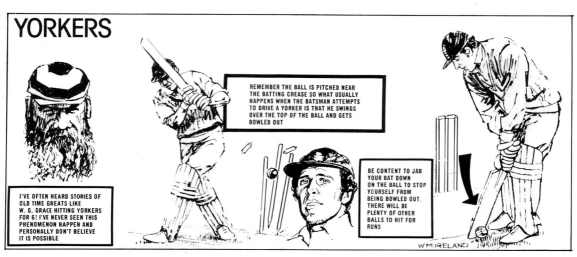

24

Test matches are no place for full tosses, especially when West Indian Alvin Kallicharran is at the receiving end. Another boundary on its way at the Oval.

Opposite above Colin Cowdrey has his own method of dealing with bouncers — not the most elegant, perhaps, but very effective. He had plenty of practice against Dennis Lillee in Perth.

Opposite below Against a bowler of John Snow's pace you have to make extra time for yourself. A short and early back-lift helps a lot.

DON'T AIM FOR SIX

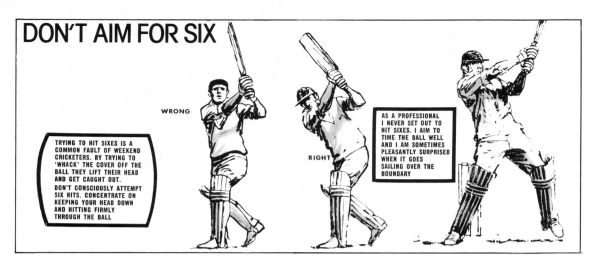

WRONG

RIGHT

TRYING TO HIT SIXES IS A COMMON FAULT OF WEEKEND CRICKETERS. BY TRYING TO 'WHACK' THE COVER OFF THE BALL THEY LIFT THEIR HEAD AND GET CAUGHT OUT.
DON'T CONSCIOUSLY ATTEMPT SIX HITS. CONCENTRATE ON KEEPING YOUR HEAD DOWN AND HITTING FIRMLY THROUGH THE BALL

AS A PROFESSIONAL I NEVER SET OUT TO HIT SIXES. I AIM TO TIME THE BALL WELL AND I AM SOMETIMES PLEASANTLY SURPRISED WHEN IT GOES SAILING OVER THE BOUNDARY

BATTING IN WINDY CONDITIONS

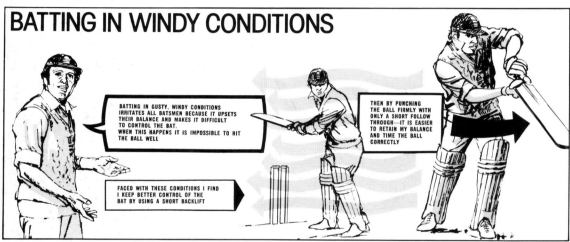

BATTING IN GUSTY, WINDY CONDITIONS IRRITATES ALL BATSMEN BECAUSE IT UPSETS THEIR BALANCE AND MAKES IT DIFFICULT TO CONTROL THE BAT.
WHEN THIS HAPPENS IT IS IMPOSSIBLE TO HIT THE BALL WELL

FACED WITH THESE CONDITIONS I FIND I KEEP BETTER CONTROL OF THE BAT BY USING A SHORT BACKLIFT

THEN BY PUNCHING THE BALL FIRMLY WITH ONLY A SHORT FOLLOW THROUGH—IT IS EASIER TO RETAIN MY BALANCE AND TIME THE BALL CORRECTLY

BATTING ON A WET PITCH

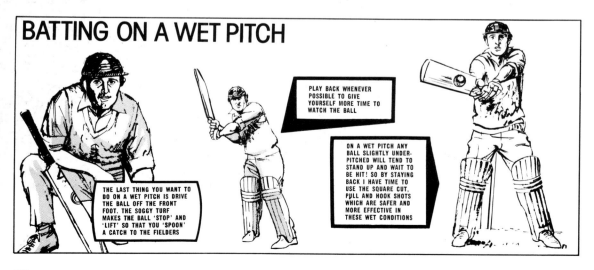

PLAY BACK WHENEVER POSSIBLE TO GIVE YOURSELF MORE TIME TO WATCH THE BALL

THE LAST THING YOU WANT TO DO ON A WET PITCH IS DRIVE THE BALL OFF THE FRONT FOOT. THE SOGGY TURF MAKES THE BALL 'STOP' AND 'LIFT' SO THAT YOU 'SPOON' A CATCH TO THE FIELDERS

ON A WET PITCH ANY BALL SLIGHTLY UNDER-PITCHED WILL TEND TO STAND UP AND WAIT TO BE HIT! SO BY STAYING BACK I HAVE TIME TO USE THE SQUARE CUT, PULL AND HOOK SHOTS WHICH ARE SAFER AND MORE EFFECTIVE IN THESE WET CONDITIONS

Timing, not brute force, is the secret of a powerful stroke.

LOSS OF FORM

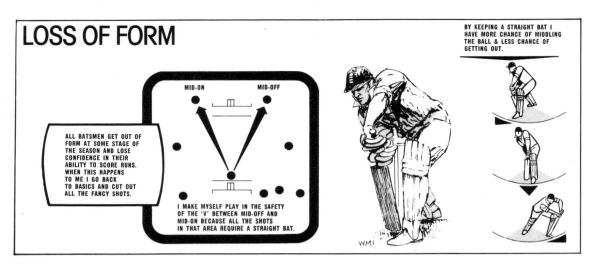

BY KEEPING A STRAIGHT BAT I HAVE MORE CHANCE OF MIDDLING THE BALL & LESS CHANCE OF GETTING OUT.

ALL BATSMEN GET OUT OF FORM AT SOME STAGE OF THE SEASON AND LOSE CONFIDENCE IN THEIR ABILITY TO SCORE RUNS. WHEN THIS HAPPENS TO ME I GO BACK TO BASICS AND CUT OUT ALL THE FANCY SHOTS.

MID-ON   MID-OFF

I MAKE MYSELF PLAY IN THE SAFETY OF THE 'V' BETWEEN MID-OFF AND MID-ON BECAUSE ALL THE SHOTS IN THAT AREA REQUIRE A STRAIGHT BAT.

PLAY YOURSELF IN

SOMETIMES BATSMEN GET OUT BECAUSE THEY TRY TO PLAY TOO MANY SHOTS AT THE BEGINNING OF THEIR INNINGS. THEY DO NOT GIVE THEMSELVES TIME TO GET USED TO THE CONDITIONS 'IN THE MIDDLE'

ALWAYS HIT THE BAD BALL. BUT WAIT UNTIL YOUR EYES GET USED TO THE LIGHT, THE BOWLER'S ACTION AND THE PACE OF THE BALL OFF THE PITCH BEFORE YOU START PLAYING ALL YOUR SHOTS

I KEEP MY SCORE 'TICKING OVER' WITH SINGLES UNTIL I FEEL CONFIDENT TO PLAY MY SHOTS

TWO SHOULDERED STANCE

FROM A NORMAL STANCE OPEN YOUR FEET AND SHOULDERS TOWARDS THE BOWLER SO THAT YOU ARE 'CHEST ON'

KEN BARRINGTON USED THIS TWO SHOULDERED STANCE TO GREAT EFFECT (THE TERM 'TWO EYED' STANCE IS INCORRECT BECAUSE BATSMEN USE BOTH EYES WHICHEVER WAY THEY STAND AT THE WICKET)

IF, AFTER A LOT OF PRACTICE YOU STILL HAVE DIFFICULTY IN DEALING WITH THE BALL PITCHED ON YOUR LEGS— DON'T PANIC—THERE IS A WAY ROUND IT

When form and confidence suffer the only way out is to start at the beginning and concentrate on playing with a straight bat. Better safe than out.

LEARN TO RELAX

THEN WHEN YOUR TURN COMES YOU WILL FIND IT EASIER BECAUSE YOU HAVE SAVED YOUR ENERGY AND DONE YOUR HOMEWORK.

MY ADVICE IS TO SIT QUIETLY AND CONCENTRATE ON THE GAME. WATCH THE OPPOSITION BOWLERS AND FIELDERS FOR ANY POINTS WHICH MAY HELP YOU WHEN YOU GO OUT TO BAT.

WHILE WAITING TO GO INTO BAT MANY PLAYERS ARE SO NERVOUS AND APPREHENSIVE THAT THEY FIDGET AND CHATTER IN THE DRESSING ROOM OFTEN TAKING LITTLE NOTICE OF THE GAME IN PROGRESS. THIS LEAVES THEM MENTALLY AND PHYSICALLY UNPREPARED FOR BATTING.

DON'T WASTE YOUR PRACTICE TIME

YOU SHOULDN'T GO TO NET PRACTICE AND JUST SLOG AWAY OR LAZE AROUND. PRACTISE INTELLIGENTLY OR YOU ARE WASTING YOUR TIME

WHEN YOU PRACTISE WITHOUT ANYTHING SPECIFIC IN MIND YOU CAN GET INTO BAD HABITS. I ASK THE BOWLERS TO BOWL SO THAT I CAN IMPROVE OR PRACTISE A PARTICULAR SHOT WHICH HAS BEEN LETTING ME DOWN IN MATCHES. IN THIS WAY I CAN IMPROVE MY BATTING AND ENJOY MY NET PRACTICE

BATTING ONE HANDED

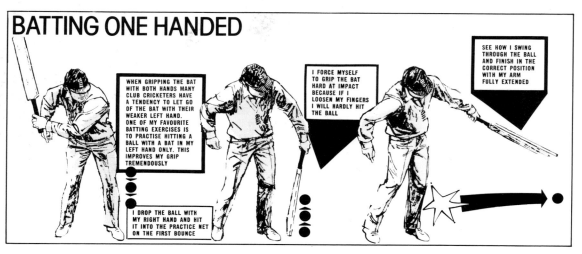

SEE HOW I SWING THROUGH THE BALL AND FINISH IN THE CORRECT POSITION WITH MY ARM FULLY EXTENDED

I FORCE MYSELF TO GRIP THE BAT HARD AT IMPACT BECAUSE IF I LOOSEN MY FINGERS I WILL HARDLY HIT THE BALL

WHEN GRIPPING THE BAT WITH BOTH HANDS MANY CLUB CRICKETERS HAVE A TENDENCY TO LET GO OF THE BAT WITH THEIR WEAKER LEFT HAND. ONE OF MY FAVOURITE BATTING EXERCISES IS TO PRACTISE HITTING A BALL WITH A BAT IN MY LEFT HAND ONLY. THIS IMPROVES MY GRIP TREMENDOUSLY

I DROP THE BALL WITH MY RIGHT HAND AND HIT IT INTO THE PRACTICE NET ON THE FIRST BOUNCE

Concentration and a sense of purpose are important in the nets, where intelligent practice can help iron out problems. I have always enjoyed practice time in the nets and tried not to waste it.

USE A LIGHTWEIGHT BAT

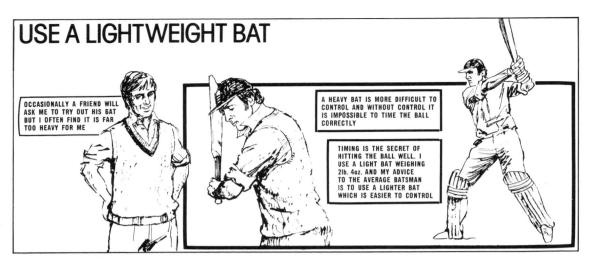

OCCASIONALLY A FRIEND WILL ASK ME TO TRY OUT HIS BAT BUT I OFTEN FIND IT IS FAR TOO HEAVY FOR ME

A HEAVY BAT IS MORE DIFFICULT TO CONTROL AND WITHOUT CONTROL IT IS IMPOSSIBLE TO TIME THE BALL CORRECTLY

TIMING IS THE SECRET OF HITTING THE BALL WELL. I USE A LIGHT BAT WEIGHING 2lb. 4oz. AND MY ADVICE TO THE AVERAGE BATSMAN IS TO USE A LIGHTER BAT WHICH IS EASIER TO CONTROL

CORRECT BAT SIZE

TO BAT WELL YOU MUST HAVE THE CORRECT SIZE BAT. MANY YOUNG PLAYERS BUY A BAT WHICH IS TOO BIG FOR THEM THINKING THEY WILL 'GROW INTO IT' AND SAVE THEMSELVES SOME MONEY. THIS SORT OF THINKING IS WRONG AS IT CREATES BAD BATTING HABITS WHICH MAY NEVER BE IRONED OUT IN LATER YEARS.

THE BEST WAY TO FIND THE RIGHT SIZE BAT IS TO TAKE UP YOUR NORMAL STANCE. THE CORRECT SIZE IS WHEN THE TOP OF THE BAT HANDLE RESTS AGAINST YOUR LEFT THIGH

IF THE BAT HANDLE RESTS ABOVE THIS POSITION—THEN THE BAT IS TOO BIG FOR YOU.

IF IT IS ESSENTIAL TO SAVE MONEY, THEN BUY A SMALL BAT. REMEMBER, EVEN SIR LEONARD HUTTON, ONE OF THE ALL TIME GREATS, USED A HARROW SIZE BAT.

CHOOSING YOUR OWN BAT

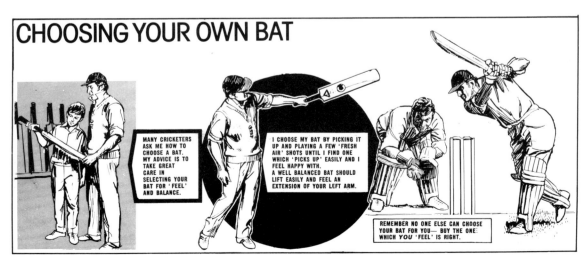

MANY CRICKETERS ASK ME HOW TO CHOOSE A BAT. MY ADVICE IS TO TAKE GREAT CARE IN SELECTING YOUR BAT FOR 'FEEL' AND BALANCE.

I CHOOSE MY BAT BY PICKING IT UP AND PLAYING A FEW 'FRESH AIR' SHOTS UNTIL I FIND ONE WHICH 'PICKS UP' EASILY AND I FEEL HAPPY WITH. A WELL BALANCED BAT SHOULD LIFT EASILY AND FEEL AN EXTENSION OF YOUR LEFT ARM.

REMEMBER NO ONE ELSE CAN CHOOSE YOUR BAT FOR YOU— BUY THE ONE: WHICH *YOU* 'FEEL' IS RIGHT.

At 6 ft 7½ ins., Tony Greig probably has more difficulty than most finding just the right equipment, but he is always careful to kit himself out properly. Remember, a bat on the small side is less of a disadvantage than one which is too big.

ARE DIRTY BATS LUCKY

NEW GRIPS FOR OLD

A BATSMAN'S EQUIPMENT

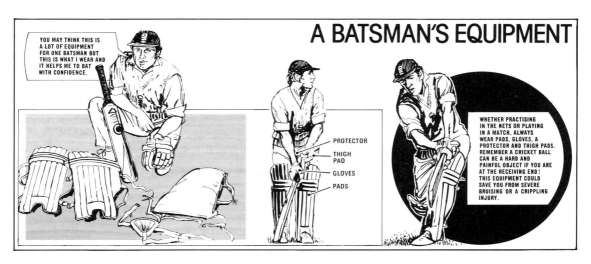

Oh dear! Either Alan Knott has a superstition about not cleaning his bat or maybe he's been using this one to dig the garden?

Bowling

With a new ball and a good bowling action any boy can learn to make the ball swing in the air and move in or out off the seam – provided he learns to grip the ball correctly.

A young bowler must make up his mind whether he wishes to bowl out-swing or in-swing and set his field accordingly. Both types of swing require different field settings so don't try to bowl both in the same over until you have got control of swing, length and direction – otherwise your bowling may prove expensive and involve risks to your close-in fielders.

Except where indicated, all the grips in this section are for right-hand bowlers. For left-hand bowlers read 'left' for 'right'.

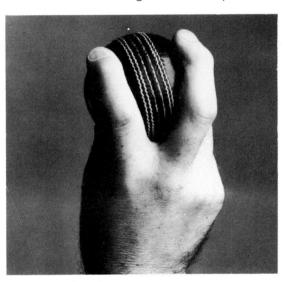

The grip for right-arm out swing

Point the seam of the ball towards the slips and place your first and second fingers on either side of the seam. Your third and fourth fingers should curve naturally down the side of the ball while your thumb rests on the seam underneath the ball.

The grip for right-arm in swing

Point the seam of the ball towards fine leg and place your first and second fingers on either side of the seam. Your second finger should lie parallel to the seam while the ball of your thumb rests on the seam underneath the ball. Let your third and fourth fingers curve naturally down the side of the ball.

Spin bowling

Although all bowlers need to concentrate on bowling good length and direction it is more important for budding spin bowlers to learn to spin the ball *first*. Experiment and then decide whether you want to be an off-spinner or a leg-spinner because it is difficult to bowl both breaks and impossible to set attacking fields for a bowler bowling both types of spin in the same over.

Leg spin

Space your first and second fingers comfortably apart *across* the seam with the top finger joints taking most of the pressure.

Your third and little fingers are naturally below them with the top joint of your third finger lying along the seam and pressing hard up against it.

Keep your wrist cocked inward and as you deliver the ball flick outward and upward with the third finger to impose spin. The action is similar to turning a door knob from right to left.

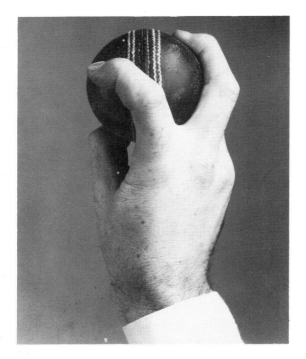 

Off spin

Grip the ball so that your first finger lies along the seam with the top joint slightly bent and biting into the near edge. This is the main finger which imparts spin.

Your second finger should be spaced comfortably but well away from the first with the other two fingers curled naturally underneath the ball. Your thumb will rest on the other side of the ball near the seam. To spin the ball rotate your hand clockwise much the same as turning the knob to open a door.

Slow left-arm

The grip for the left-arm orthodox slow or slow medium bowler is the same as for the right-arm off-spin bowler, except in reverse, so to speak. Follow the instructions given for the off-spin grip, but note that your hand will rotate in an anti-clockwise direction.

Accuracy, control and infinite variety are the hallmark of three of the greatest bowlers in the world. Bishen Bedi *top left* slow left-arm bowler of Northants and India; Gary Sobers *top right* who could bowl above medium pace or turn his fingers to left-arm spin; and Intikhab Alam *below* whose leg breaks test the ability of the most capable batsmen.

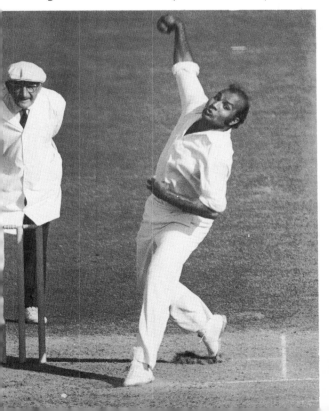

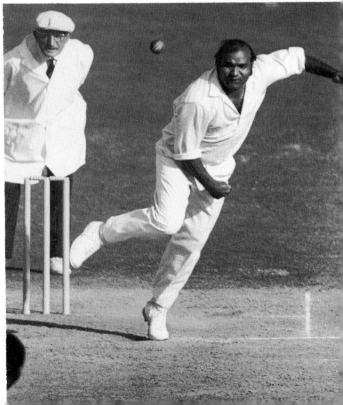

BASIC BOWLING ACTION 1

BASIC BOWLING ACTION 2

GREAT BOWLERS USE THEIR HEADS

42

Generating speed and accuracy is not just a matter of racing to the wicket and throwing yourself into a delivery. A good bowling action is progressive and controlled, whether the classic cartwheel action of John Snow *above* or the explosive style of Dennis Lillee *below left* and Mike Procter.

BOWLING FOR BEGINNERS

BOWLING IS NOT A NATURAL ACTION LIKE THROWING, BUT EVERY SMALL BOY CAN LEARN TO BOWL WELL ENOUGH TO ENJOY HIMSELF IF HE FOLLOWS THIS SIMPLE EXERCISE.

STAND WITH YOUR FEET ASTRIDE AND ARMS SIDEWAYS. THEN ROCK FROM ONE FOOT TO THE OTHER KEEPING YOUR ARMS OUTSTRETCHED.

CONTINUE ROCKING WITH YOUR ARMS SWINGING LOOSELY LIKE THE SAILS OF A WINDMILL.

NOW DO THIS WITH THE BALL IN YOUR HAND AND AFTER ROCKING A FEW TIMES, LET THE BALL GO. YOU ARE NOW BOWLING.

LEARN TO BOWL STRAIGHT

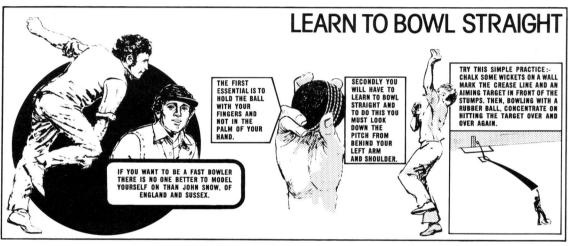

THE FIRST ESSENTIAL IS TO HOLD THE BALL WITH YOUR FINGERS AND NOT IN THE PALM OF YOUR HAND.

IF YOU WANT TO BE A FAST BOWLER THERE IS NO ONE BETTER TO MODEL YOURSELF ON THAN JOHN SNOW, OF ENGLAND AND SUSSEX.

SECONDLY YOU WILL HAVE TO LEARN TO BOWL STRAIGHT AND TO DO THIS YOU MUST LOOK DOWN THE PITCH FROM BEHIND YOUR LEFT ARM AND SHOULDER.

TRY THIS SIMPLE PRACTICE:- CHALK SOME WICKETS ON A WALL MARK THE CREASE LINE AND AN AIMING TARGET IN FRONT OF THE STUMPS. THEN, BOWLING WITH A RUBBER BALL, CONCENTRATE ON HITTING THE TARGET OVER AND OVER AGAIN.

DON'T WASTE THE NEW BALL

IT IS A BOWLING 'CRIME' TO WASTE THE NEW BALL BY BOWLING WIDE OF THE STUMPS SO THAT THE BATSMAN DOES NOT HAVE TO PLAY A SHOT

WHEN I OPEN AN INNINGS I AM DELIGHTED IF I DON'T HAVE TO PLAY THE NEW BALL MUCH IN THE FIRST FEW OVERS. IT GIVES ME A CHANCE TO SETTLE DOWN AND GET USED TO THE CONDITIONS WHILE THE SHINE IS GOING OFF THE BALL AND THE BOWLER TIRES—ALL TO NO PURPOSE

AT THE START OF AN INNINGS THE ADVANTAGE LIES WITH THE NEW BALL BOWLER—NOT THE BATSMAN. THE BOWLER MUST RETAIN HIS ADVANTAGE BY BOWLING STRAIGHT ENOUGH TO MAKE THE BATSMAN PLAY

A vote of thanks to the bowler . . . but not from this close fielder who has to take evasive action as Ray Illingworth sweeps a loose delivery. Bowl straight if you want to stay friends with your own team-mates.

Nasty, but not particularly effective. A batsman facing the new ball should be made to play every delivery; pace is no substitute for accuracy.

BOWLING AGAINST THE WIND

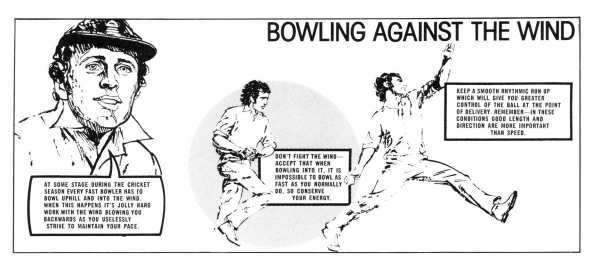

AT SOME STAGE DURING THE CRICKET SEASON EVERY FAST BOWLER HAS TO BOWL UPHILL AND INTO THE WIND. WHEN THIS HAPPENS IT'S JOLLY HARD WORK WITH THE WIND BLOWING YOU BACKWARDS AS YOU USELESSLY STRIVE TO MAINTAIN YOUR PACE.

DON'T FIGHT THE WIND—ACCEPT THAT WHEN BOWLING INTO IT, IT IS IMPOSSIBLE TO BOWL AS FAST AS YOU NORMALLY DO, SO CONSERVE YOUR ENERGY.

KEEP A SMOOTH RHYTHMIC RUN UP WHICH WILL GIVE YOU GREATER CONTROL OF THE BALL AT THE POINT OF DELIVERY. REMEMBER—IN THESE CONDITIONS GOOD LENGTH AND DIRECTION ARE MORE IMPORTANT THAN SPEED.

BOWLING AT TALL MEN

ONCE YOU CAN BOWL GOOD LENGTH BALLS YOU MUST LEARN TO VARY YOUR LENGTH ACCORDING TO THE BATSMAN.

WHEN BOWLING TO A TALL BATSMAN SUCH AS WEST INDIAN CLIVE LLOYD AN ORDINARY LENGTH BALL BECOMES A HALF VOLLEY AND IS HIT FOR FOUR. HIS EXTRA HEIGHT MEANS HE HAS AN ENORMOUSLY LONG STRIDE AND HE GETS NEARER TO THE PITCH OF THE BALL THAN MOST BATSMEN.

IN THIS SITUATION YOU MUST MAKE IT DIFFICULT FOR THE TALL BATSMAN TO SCORE RUNS BY SHORTENING YOUR LENGTH AND UNDER PITCHING CONSIDERABLY.

EXPERIMENT IN THE NETS

AT NET PRACTICE BATSMEN TEND TO THINK BOWLERS ARE ONLY THERE TO HELP THEM IMPROVE THEIR BATTING THEY COULDN'T BE MORE WRONG!

WATCH THE ENGLAND BOWLERS AT THE NETS. THEY SPEND THE TIME TRYING OUT VARIATIONS TO ADD TO THEIR BOWLING ARMOURY. NEXT TIME YOU GO TO PRACTISE, EXPERIMENT. TRY SOMETHING NEW BY ATTEMPTING TO BOWL A YORKER, A SLOWER BALL, A BOUNCER, OR EVEN TRY BOWLING ROUND THE WICKET.

IN THE NETS JOHN SNOW OFTEN BOWLS AT ONE STUMP TO HELP HIM ACHIEVE GREATER ACCURACY

The sort of thing that can happen if a bowler misjudges his length against a batsman as tall as Clive Lloyd. Dennis Lillee tried to dig in a bouncer in the World Cup final – and Clive punished him unmercifully.

Fielding

Opposite How's that for concentration. India's Venkat watches the ball right into his hands to account for John Jameson in a World Cup tie at Lord's and Chris Old swoops to take a two-handed catch to dismiss Max Walker in the Headingley Test match.

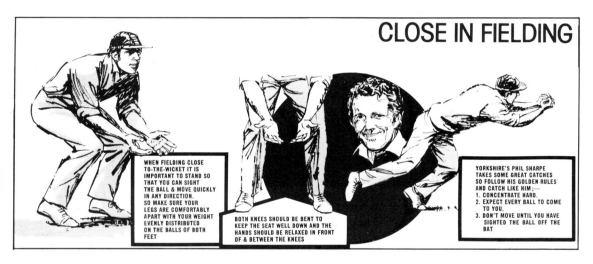

CLOSE IN FIELDING

WHEN FIELDING CLOSE TO-THE-WICKET IT IS IMPORTANT TO STAND SO THAT YOU CAN SIGHT THE BALL & MOVE QUICKLY IN ANY DIRECTION. SO MAKE SURE YOUR LEGS ARE COMFORTABLY APART WITH YOUR WEIGHT EVENLY DISTRIBUTED ON THE BALLS OF BOTH FEET

BOTH KNEES SHOULD BE BENT TO KEEP THE SEAT WELL DOWN AND THE HANDS SHOULD BE RELAXED IN FRONT OF & BETWEEN THE KNEES

YORKSHIRE'S PHIL SHARPE TAKES SOME GREAT CATCHES SO FOLLOW HIS GOLDEN RULES AND CATCH LIKE HIM;—
1. CONCENTRATE HARD.
2. EXPECT EVERY BALL TO COME TO YOU.
3. DON'T MOVE UNTIL YOU HAVE SIGHTED THE BALL OFF THE BAT

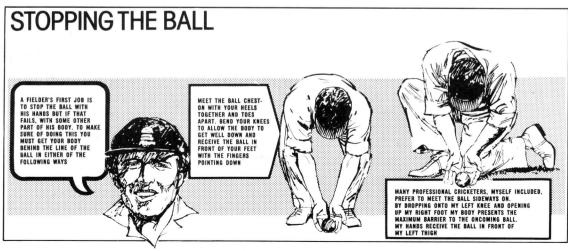

STOPPING THE BALL

A FIELDER'S FIRST JOB IS TO STOP THE BALL WITH HIS HANDS BUT IF THAT FAILS, WITH SOME OTHER PART OF HIS BODY. TO MAKE SURE OF DOING THIS YOU MUST GET YOUR BODY BEHIND THE LINE OF THE BALL IN EITHER OF THE FOLLOWING WAYS

MEET THE BALL CHEST-ON WITH YOUR HEELS TOGETHER AND TOES APART. BEND YOUR KNEES TO ALLOW THE BODY TO GET WELL DOWN AND RECEIVE THE BALL IN FRONT OF YOUR FEET WITH THE FINGERS POINTING DOWN

MANY PROFESSIONAL CRICKETERS, MYSELF INCLUDED, PREFER TO MEET THE BALL SIDEWAYS ON. BY DROPPING ONTO MY LEFT KNEE AND OPENING UP MY RIGHT FOOT MY BODY PRESENTS THE MAXIMUM BARRIER TO THE ONCOMING BALL. MY HANDS RECEIVE THE BALL IN FRONT OF MY LEFT THIGH

ATTACKING FIELDING-THE PICK UP

ATTACKING FIELDING-THE THROW IN

Opposite Run if you dare when Alvin Kallicharran is the fielder. Kalli is perfectly positioned for a hard return from the moment he picks up the ball and a quick accurate throw deters many batsmen from trying for that extra run.

HIGH CATCHES

GIVE YOURSELF ROOM

CATCHING A HARD ONE

It looks easy for Rick McCosker after a delivery lobs high off Colin Cowdrey's gloves but he is rightly taking no chances. Hands together, fingers spread, eyes fixed on the ball – no escape for Colin. And none for Jeff Thomson *below* brilliantly caught by Chris Old on one of those occasions when good positioning and quick reflexes produce the impossible.

PRACTICE AT PLAYTIME

EVERY BOY CAN IMPROVE HIS 'BALL SENSE' IF HE IS KEEN ENOUGH. HERE IS A SIMPLE EXAMPLE OF HOW TO IMPROVE YOUR CATCHING AND THROWING

IF YOU ARE AT A 'LOOSE END' ON YOUR OWN CHALK A TARGET ON A WALL. STAND A FEW YARDS AWAY AND THROW A RUBBER BALL AT THE TARGET —CATCHING IT AS IT BOUNCES BACK

IF YOU HAVE A FRIEND WILLING TO PLAY WITH YOU STAND A FEW YARDS APART FACING THE WALL. USING THE SAME TARGET THROW AND CATCH THE BALL IN TURN

TO IMPROVE YOUR SLIP FIELDING AND QUICKEN YOUR REACTIONS TRY THIS GAME. 2 BOYS FACE A WALL AT A DISTANCE OF SOME 4 TO 5 YARDS. A 3RD. BOY STANDS BEHIND THEM AND THROWS A RUBBER BALL AT THE WALL. THE 2 BOYS FACING THE WALL HAVE TO SIGHT AND CATCH THE BALL ON THE REBOUND

FIELDING CAN BE FUN

FIELDING IS THE EASIEST AND MOST NATURAL OF ALL CRICKET ACTIVITIES. BUT YOU CAN'T CALL YOURSELF A CRICKETER UNTIL YOU ARE A GOOD FIELDER

HAVE A BIT OF FIELDING PRACTICE IN FRONT OF THE PAVILION BEFORE THE START OF EVERY MATCH. EVEN TEST CRICKETERS HAVE A FEW MINUTES WARM UP BEFORE THEY TAKE THE FIELD. IT GIVES THEM A CHANCE TO GET THE FEEL OF THE BALL

WHEN YOUR TEAM TAKES THE FIELD DON'T TREAT IT AS A CHORE—GO OUT MEANING TO ENJOY YOURSELF. GOOD FIELDING WILL INSPIRE YOUR TEAM AND HELP THE BOWLERS BY SAVING RUNS AND CREATING A RUN OUT

CRICKET FOR EVERY BOY

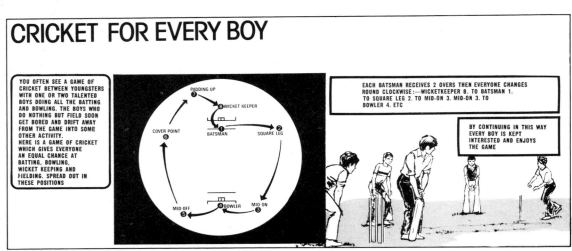

YOU OFTEN SEE A GAME OF CRICKET BETWEEN YOUNGSTERS WITH ONE OR TWO TALENTED BOYS DOING ALL THE BATTING AND BOWLING. THE BOYS WHO DO NOTHING BUT FIELD SOON GET BORED AND DRIFT AWAY FROM THE GAME INTO SOME OTHER ACTIVITY.
HERE IS A GAME OF CRICKET WHICH GIVES EVERYONE AN EQUAL CHANCE AT BATTING, BOWLING, WICKET KEEPING AND FIELDING. SPREAD OUT IN THESE POSITIONS

7 PADDING UP
8 WICKET KEEPER
1 BATSMAN
2 SQUARE LEG
6 COVER POINT
5 MID OFF
4 BOWLER
3 MID ON

EACH BATSMAN RECEIVES 2 OVERS THEN EVERYONE CHANGES ROUND CLOCKWISE:—WICKETKEEPER 8. TO BATSMAN 1. TO SQUARE LEG 2. TO MID-ON 3. MID-ON 3. TO BOWLER 4. ETC

BY CONTINUING IN THIS WAY EVERY BOY IS KEPT INTERESTED AND ENJOYS THE GAME

One of the greatest fielders in the world, Clive Lloyd's keen eye enables him to pick up one-handed if necessary and his sharpness, suppleness and sense of balance produce extraordinary feats of fielding. Reliable and aggressive, his presence alone must have been worth hundreds of runs to Lancashire and West Indies.

Captaincy

Captaincy has been described as a gift, an acquired skill, an art and a science, but whichever way you look at it, captaincy plays an important and sometimes vital role in cricket.

When a side wins a captain is not usually given special credit; if a side loses it is not uncommon for the captain to be blamed. Human nature being what it is nobody wants to admit to playing badly, so everybody tends to look for a scapegoat – and the captain can come under fire from batsmen, bowlers and fielders alike. Even spectators usually reckon they could have done a better job, so don't expect too much credit for your efforts.

Because of this there may be a tendency to try to please everybody – but resist it. Too much well meaning advice from your players and outsiders can only complicate matters for you. If you are going to take responsibility for decisions do yourself justice by making them yourself. In other words, have the courage of your convictions.

That does not mean you cannot benefit from the experience and knowledge of others. When you feel it necessary, confer with your vice-captain and accept a little help from your players. You are always learning at this game and a captain has to be willing to learn faster and more often than any of

When West Indies attack – they do it in style. Rohan Kanhai, one of the shrewdest of captains, pressures Derek Underwood at Lord's in 1973. All eleven West Indies players are grouped in the picture.

Field setting

Out-swing, right arm

(a) Good pitch

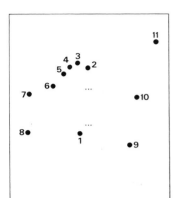

1. Bowler
2. Wicket-keeper
3. First slip
4. Second slip
5. Third slip
6. Gully
7. Square cover-point
8. Wide mid-off – more or less extra cover
9. Mid-on
10. Square leg
11. Fine leg

(b) Slow or wet pitch, with the occasional ball 'stopping'

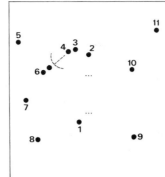

1. Bowler
2. Wicket-keeper
3. First slip
4. Second slip would stay there or move to second gully depending on the wishes of the bowler
5. Third slip to third man
6. Gully
7. Square cover would move to a more orthodox cover position in front of the wicket
8. Mid-off would move straight
9. Mid-on
10. Square leg to backward short leg to catch the occasional ball which 'stops' or 'pops'
11. Fine leg

In-swing, right arm

(a) Good pitch

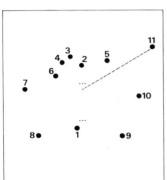

1. Bowler
2. Wicket-keeper
3. First slip
4. Second slip
5. Leg slip
6. Gully
7. Cover point in front of square
8. Straight mid-off
9. Mid-on
10. Square leg
11. Fine leg *wide* of leg slip

(b) Slow or wet pitch with the occasional ball 'stopping'

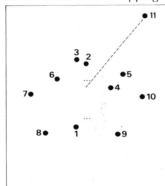

1. Bowler
2. Wicket-keeper
3. First slip
4. Second slip would go to short square leg } Both to catch the ball which lifts off a length
5. Leg slip would go square or wider }
6. Gully
7. Cover point in front of square
8. Straight mid-off
9. Mid-on
10. Square leg
11. Fine leg would move finer or 'inside' the leg slip

Left-arm swing bowling over the wicket

(a) Good pitch – new ball, attacking field

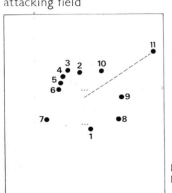

1. Bowler
2. Wicket-keeper
3. First slip
4. Second slip
5. Wide third slip
6. Gully
7. Extra cover or wide mid-off saving the single
8. Wide mid-on or straightish mid-wicket saving the single
9. Square leg
10. Leg slip
11. Fine leg outside leg slip

(b) Slow or wet pitch – occasional ball 'stopping'

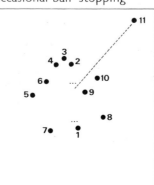

1. Bowler
2. Wicket-keeper
3. First slip
4. Second slip
5. Third slip to cover
6. Gully
7. Extra cover moves straighter to mid-off
8. Wide mid-on or straightish mid-wicket saving the single
9. Square leg to short square leg
10. Leg slip moves squarer or wider
11. Fine leg moves finer or 'inside' the leg slip

his players. But a captain has to be positive and decisive, even when there are half a dozen awkward factors which have to be weighed in his decision.

If you don't always feel absolutely certain that your decision is right – and that is bound to happen if you are honest with yourself – at least look and act in a positive fashion. Keep a cool head, don't get ruffled or show you are worried and above all don't change your mind with every delivery or the team will soon become uncertain and lose confidence in you.

On the other hand a captain has to be flexible, to keep an open mind and try to suit his tactics to a game that can change by the minute. It is not a crime to change your mind, provided that you think changes through and don't make them in an atmosphere of panic.

Always give encouragement when you feel it is due, although sooner or later you will have to be critical of the team and individual performances. That is inevitable and an important part of any captain's responsibilities.

Try to be constructive in your criticism, remembering that individuals are likely to react in different ways. Don't be afraid to be forceful when a point has to be made but guard against the kind of criticism which makes a player feel resentful.

Study the personalities in your own team as closely as you study the opposition's strengths and weaknesses. Your technical ability as a captain is entirely a matter of your own performance and experience but you can become a really good leader if you discover how to make a team work together.

It's a difficult job for which there is no easy formula, no straightforward method which any textbook can teach. It's very much up to you.

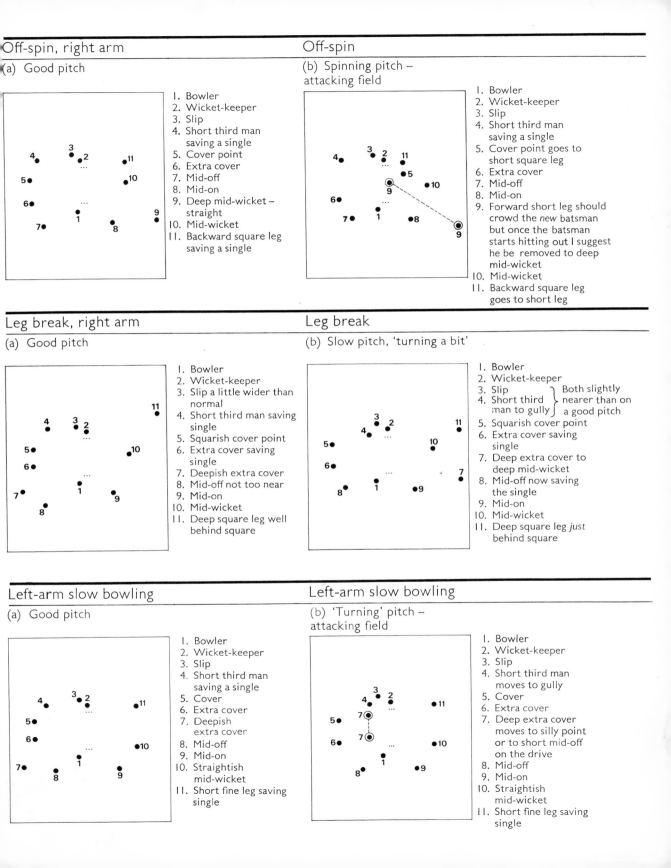

Off-spin, right arm

(a) Good pitch

1. Bowler
2. Wicket-keeper
3. Slip
4. Short third man saving a single
5. Cover point
6. Extra cover
7. Mid-off
8. Mid-on
9. Deep mid-wicket – straight
10. Mid-wicket
11. Backward square leg saving a single

Off-spin

(b) Spinning pitch – attacking field

1. Bowler
2. Wicket-keeper
3. Slip
4. Short third man saving a single
5. Cover point goes to short square leg
6. Extra cover
7. Mid-off
8. Mid-on
9. Forward short leg should crowd the *new* batsman but once the batsman starts hitting out I suggest he be removed to deep mid-wicket
10. Mid-wicket
11. Backward square leg goes to short leg

Leg break, right arm

(a) Good pitch

1. Bowler
2. Wicket-keeper
3. Slip a little wider than normal
4. Short third man saving single
5. Squarish cover point
6. Extra cover saving single
7. Deepish extra cover
8. Mid-off not too near
9. Mid-on
10. Mid-wicket
11. Deep square leg well behind square

Leg break

(b) Slow pitch, 'turning a bit'

1. Bowler
2. Wicket-keeper
3. Slip } Both slightly
4. Short third } nearer than on man to gully } a good pitch
5. Squarish cover point
6. Extra cover saving single
7. Deep extra cover to deep mid-wicket
8. Mid-off now saving the single
9. Mid-on
10. Mid-wicket
11. Deep square leg *just* behind square

Left-arm slow bowling

(a) Good pitch

1. Bowler
2. Wicket-keeper
3. Slip
4. Short third man saving a single
5. Cover
6. Extra cover
7. Deepish extra cover
8. Mid-off
9. Mid-on
10. Straightish mid-wicket
11. Short fine leg saving single

Left-arm slow bowling

(b) 'Turning' pitch – attacking field

1. Bowler
2. Wicket-keeper
3. Slip
4. Short third man moves to gully
5. Cover
6. Extra cover
7. Deep extra cover moves to silly point or to short mid-off on the drive
8. Mid-off
9. Mid-on
10. Straightish mid-wicket
11. Short fine leg saving single

Wicket-keeping

Alan Knott, one of the best and most experienced wicket-keepers in the world, says: 'Wicket-keeping is hard work but wonderfully rewarding because you are never out of the game.'

There are two chief essentials for keeping wicket – an ability to sight the ball early and then to catch it, whether it comes from a ball bowled, a hit or a throw-in.

On taking the ball you must 'give' a little with the hands, reducing resistance and the risk of the ball jumping out of the gloves. This 'give' also helps prevent bruising. Relax your hands and try not to keep the fingers rigid; they should form a padded cup into which the ball will sink.

Dismiss from your mind any thought that the ball is going to hit the wicket, the batsman's body or even go for runs, and build up your powers of concentration to the point where you believe and expect every ball is coming through to you.

Equipment

The most important part of any wicket-keeper's equipment is obviously his gloves, and the choice is a matter of personal preference. Some keepers like a supple pair with hardly any cushioning so that they feel the ball as much as possible; others prefer a heavy, well-padded pair for protection. Use the ones with which you feel happy and comfortable.

Whichever you choose I advise all youngsters to use a pair of cotton or chamois inners. Dampen them to make them pliable but don't over-soak them. They make for more comfort and may prevent your hands becoming bruised which is absolutely essential. If your hands do become bruised you may reach a point where you do not want the ball to come to you and that is a hopeless situation.

Finally, always wear an abdominal protector: it's the common-sense way to avoid a serious injury.

Stance

While waiting for the ball to be delivered most keepers place their hands on the ground between their legs, others rest them on their knees and some, including Yorkshire's David Bairstow, have their fingers resting on the ground outside their legs.

There is no hard and fast rule; try each position to see which one suits you and adopt the one which feels most comfortable. You may be out in the field for very long periods so comfort is essential. Keep your weight distributed evenly on the balls of both feet so you can move quickly in either direction and try not to tilt your head in order to see the ball. If you look at the ball with your head steady and your eyes level you will focus much better.

If you think you can reach it – go for it. Rodney Marsh (above) did and that's the end of Tony Greig in the World Cup semi-final at Headingley. Concentration is a basic essential to sound wicket-keeping and England's Alan Knott is typically alert and involved even though Ross Edwards has forced the ball away.

Standing back

Most keepers like to take the ball about waist height and that determines how far back they stand. The aim should be to take a good-length ball just after it begins to drop in its trajectory towards you after pitching.

Position yourself wide of the off stump so you can see the ball all the way from the bowler's hand; don't tuck yourself too far behind the stumps or you will not see balls pitching on the leg stump because of the batsman's body.

A wicket-keeper standing back must always be ready to go for any catch he reckons he can take, boldly and without hesitation. And that applies regardless of the position of the slips.

Standing up

Most young wicket-keepers feel a bit apprehensive about standing up to the wicket in case the ball is deflected sharply and hits them. That is perfectly understandable but with practice and concentration there is no real need to worry.

Squat down so that your view is not restricted by the batsman's body and keep your head as close to the line of the off stump as possible – the closer the better. Then you will have a good view and be in a position to whip off the bails without stretching or the need for a short pace, which costs valuable time if a stumping chance comes along. Obviously, you should not be so close to the stumps that your movement is restricted by them.

Typical of Alan Knott *below left* an acrobatic leap to retrieve a bad return, *below and opposite above* perfect positioning in the belief that every delivery is going to come through to him and *opposite below* a quicksilver stumping off a delivery which bounced and turned.